*To my mom:*

- - - - - - - - - - - - - - - - -

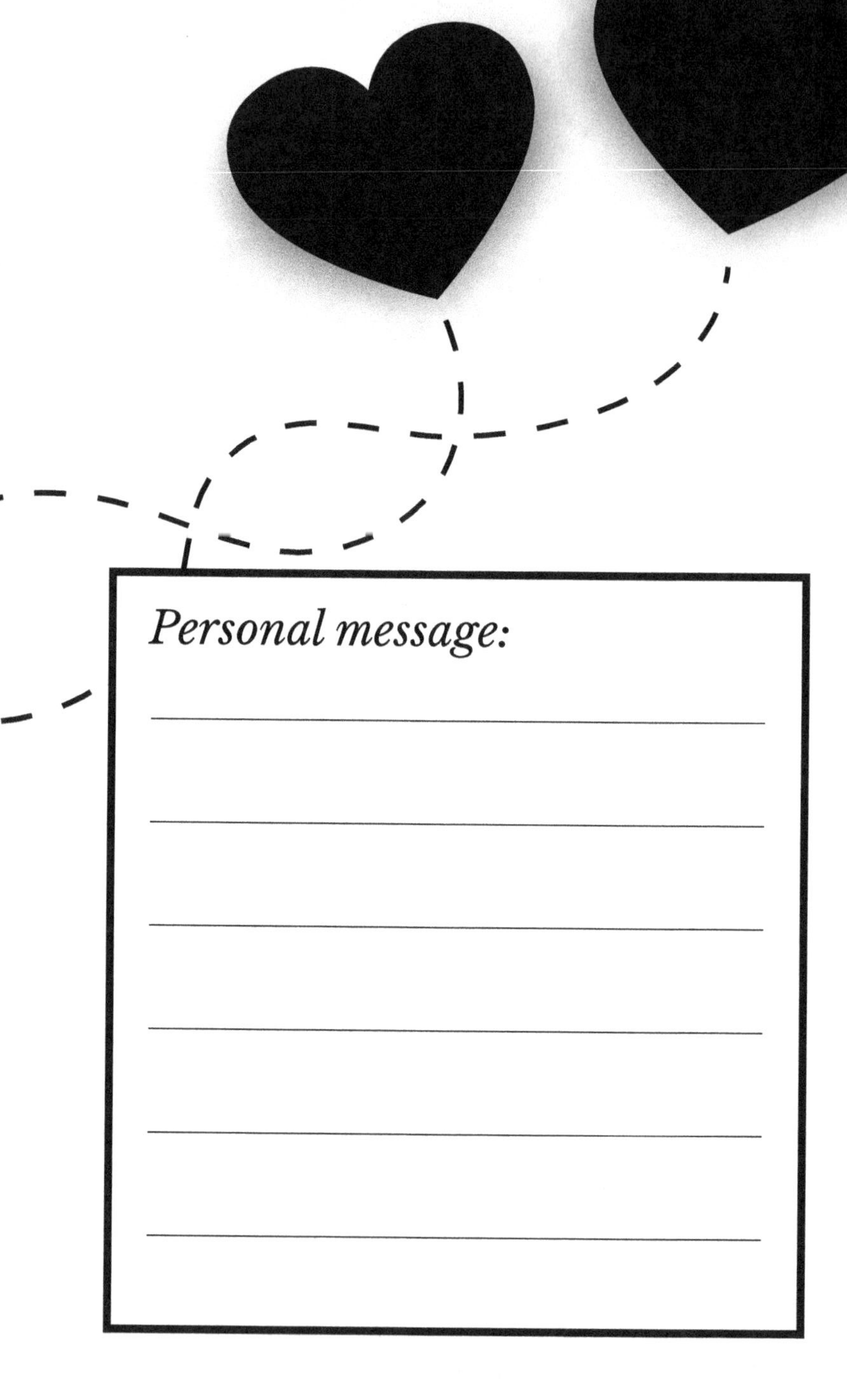

Personal message:

# 1

*I love your*

------------------------------

# 2

*You are my favorite*

------

*in the world.*

# 3

*I love hearing stories
about your*

----------------------------------

# 4

*I love how talented*
*you are at*

---

# 5

*When we are apart,
it makes me happy
to think about*

# 6

*I believe we'd make a great*

-------------------------------

*team*

# 7

*I love to hear you yelling*

----------------------------------

*at dad*

# 8

*You deserve the*

---

*award*

# 9

*I love the sound of your*

- - - - - - - - - - - - - - - - - - - - - - - - - - - - - - - - - -

*when you*

- - - - - - - - - - - - - - - - - - - - - - - - - - - - - - - -

# 10

*If you were a holiday,
you'd be*

- - - - - - - - - - - - - - - - - - - - - - - - - - - - - -

# 11

*It's hard to put into words
how strongly I feel
about your*

- - - - - - - - - - - - - - - - - - - - - - - - -

# 12

*I love how good you are
at giving me*

---------------------------------------

# 13

*Your favorite swear word*

-------------------------------------------

# 14

*I love when you make*

---

# 15

*I love going to*

- - - - - - - - - - - - - - - - - - - - - - - - - - - - - - - - - - -

*with you*

# 16

*I love to hug you when*

- - - - - - - - - - - - - - - - - - - - - - - - - - - - - - - - -

# 17

*You have
the greatest taste in*

---

# 18

*I love how you*

- - - - - - - - - - - - - - - - - - - - - - - - - - - - - - - - -

*every day*

# 19

*If you wanted to,
you could easily*

# 20

*You make me want to be
a better*

-----------------------------------------

# 21

*I would love to create a*

- - - - - - - - - - - - - - - - - - - - - - - - - - -

*for you*

# 22

*I love to play*

- - - - - - - - - - - - - - - - - - - - - - - - - - -

*with you*

# 23

*I believe the world
needs your unique*

- - - - - - - - - - - - - - - - - - - - - - - - - - - -

# 24

*I am so*

- - - - - - - - - - - - - - - - - - - - - - - - - - - - - - - -

*that you're my mom*

# 25

We should totally

_____________________________

together

# 26

*I love when you try to*

-----------------------------------

# 27

*If you were a color,
you'd be*

# 28

*I still can't believe you*

- - - - - - - - - - - - - - - - - - - - - - - - - -

# 29

*I love when you*

---

*to*

---

# 30

*It is so incredibly
funny when you*

------------------------------

# 31

*You are so*

------------------------------

*after a movie*

# 32

*You give the best*

-------------------------------------

# 33

*I love remembering
the time when*

---

# 34

*I love when you*

_________________________________________________

# 35

Everyone should be as

_______________________________

as you

# 36

*I love it when you*

---

*like*

---

# 37

*I never get tired of your*

- - - - - - - - - - - - - - - - - - - - - - - - - - - -

# 38

*I love how
you never get tired of my*

- - - - - - - - - - - - - - - - - - - - - - - - - - - - - - - - - - - - - - -

# 39

*I love to*

----------------------------------

*for you*

# 40

*Your best dance move*

-----------------------------

# 41

*When you cry I*

# 42

*I love when we*

- - - - - - - - - - - - - - - - - - - - - - - - - - - - -

*together*

# 43

*If you were a dessert,
you'd be*

- - - - - - - - - - - - - - - - - - - - - - - - - - - - - - - - - -

# 44

*I always want to hear what you're going to say about*

# 45

*I love how passionate
you are about*

----------------------------

# 46

*I love how you believe in*

- - - - - - - - - - - - - - - - - - - - - - - - - - - - - - - - - - - - - - - -

# 47

*You are so obsessed
about*

- - - - - - - - - - - - - - - - - - - - - - - - - - - - - - - - - - - - -

# 48

*I love how you
drive the*

----------------------------------------

# 49

Nobody else can

---

like you

# 50

*I'm so*

------------------------------

*that*

------------------------------

"I love u
MOM"